RIGGED

How the establishment
controls elections and how the citizens
can take them back

Ted Stevenot

Dedicated to Ohio's liberty movement.

Contents

Foreword

The first thing you're told when you get involved in politics is that 'elections matter.'

And, sure, that's true.

But, it's only after you get really involved in politics that you realize, winning the general election alone isn't enough.

When you take a look at a congressional 'score card' and see that your congressman voted for the TARP bailouts, NSA funding, or for the CROMNIBUS, you realize the system is more than a little bit rigged.

Fortunately for us, the status quo looks like it may be starting to break down. In September 2015, Speaker of the House, John Boehner announced his resignation in the middle of his term. This happened just a year after Dave Brat, a totally unknown political activist, unseated the House Majority Leader Eric Cantor. Both of these events handed virtually unprecedented defeats to the political establishment.

Yet, as great as those wins were, we are never going to see lasting change without gaining more say in the behind-the-scenes political process. As Ted Stevenot explains in this book, elections may matter - *but it is the local political parties and the primaries that rule.*

Only if we engage the system from the ground up - beginning with individual precincts - can we actually begin to push back the political establishment that has dominated our nation's politics for the past century.

Precinct by precinct, county by county, we are going to take our country back. And when we have done that, we can make a real difference in who we send to Washington.

I hope you will join *FreedomWorks* and Ohio Rising in supporting the Ohio Precinct Project. With your help in this vital effort, we can ignite true change in the direction of our country.

Noah Wall
National Director of Grassroots
FreedomWorks

Introduction

In 2014, Congress had an approval rating of 13%. Yet, in November of that same year, over 96% of Congressional representatives were reelected.

Citizen dissatisfaction with government, elected officials, and the political parties is at an all-time high. This has led to tea parties, rallies, phone calls, petitions, protests, letters to the editor, bumper stickers, yard signs, "Don't Tread on Me" flags, marches on DC, and even a few votes to usher in "new" Congressional leadership.

But little has changed.

Government continues to grow at breakneck pace. The national debt is now $18.3 trillion and climbing. The labor participation rate is at a 38 year low. Citizen dependence on safety-net entitlements has reached historic levels. And, in perhaps the most egregious example of top-down political usurpation in American history, the Affordable Care Act, a policy impacting 1/6th of our nation's economy *that at no point has had a majority of support*, is being rammed down the people's throats.

What has happened to our country?

How can politicians be so unpopular yet still manage to

overwhelmingly win reelection? How can our representatives get away with campaigning to repeal programs like Obamacare, yet fully fund such programs once elected? How can the rule of law and our Constitution be so brazenly trampled time and time again without consequence? How can government agencies target citizens for their political views with no recourse? "Uh...the hard drives crashed." Seriously?

The list goes on and on...

Even more fundamentally, *why doesn't the voice of the people seem to matter anymore?* Why can't the citizens successfully elect new representatives who could put a stop to this insanity and begin correcting our nation's course?

Because the system is rigged.

The unspoken truth is that the people have lost control of the process of deciding who represents them in government. And, in turn, they have lost control of the direction of the country.

I will show, in the pages that follow, how small groups of local and loosely affiliated establishment operatives have gained control of our country's candidate selection process. They use this process to promote their own self-interests rather than uphold and protect the people's liberty.

As a consequence, they have co-opted the citizens' ability to advance principled representatives to public office and to hold government accountable. This usurps the will of the people and ensures that crony, pro-establishment, and big-government operatives maintain control.

This is not a conspiracy theory.

It is, instead, a simple revelation that the true party establishment is made up of *hundreds of local individuals guided by an invisible hand of self-interest and corruption*. The system, in its present condition, provides little incentive for these individuals to stand up for the rights or the liberty of the people they ostensibly swear to serve.

But, the good news is, this problem can be solved.

It is well within the reach of regular citizens to reverse the status quo. Doing so requires fewer people, less time, less money, and less effort than protesting, boycotting, rallying, writing letters to the editor, or begging corrupt elected officials to do the right thing.

Part 1: How Elections are Rigged

On the next page is a graph I use in presentations to explain how small groups of insiders have the power to determine who gets elected in most races (especially U.S. House, state house, and state senate, but in many other races as well). Once it "clicks" and people see what the graph is really saying, I have even heard audible gasps from the crowd.

An unusual reaction from a simple graph...

The graph depicts numbers from the 2014 primary election in my home county of Clermont, Ohio.

If you come to understand this graph and what it is truly revealing, you will likely never look at elections or the political parties in the same way again. But, along with this new perspective, you will see a clear path for the people to reclaim our political system from the cronies and restore it to health.

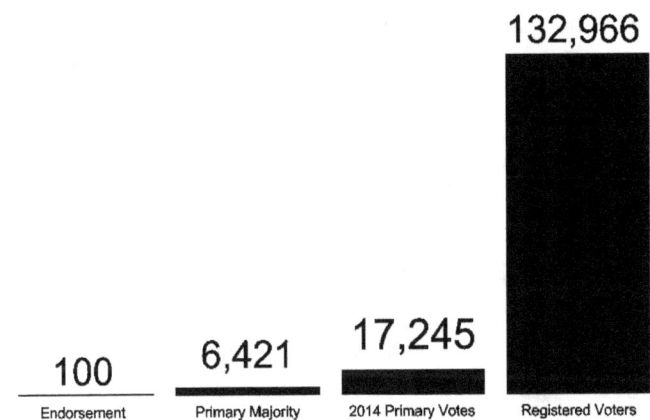

			132,966
100	6,421	17,245	
Endorsement	Primary Majority	2014 Primary Votes	Registered Voters

The graph explained

The first important fact to note is that Clermont is a "Republican" county. No Democrat has won a partisan race here for decades. This built in one-sidedness is _not unique and resembles nearly 80% of U.S. Congressional Districts._ In the last redistricting, effectively all of Ohio's Congressional districts were drawn or "gerrymandered" to be controlled by one or the other major political party.

Due to this lopsided one-party dominance, attempting to elect a new, non-incumbent representative in the general election (i.e. November) is all but impossible. In such areas, _the only opportunity to make a change is the primary election._

- The "**fourth**" column on the graph (far right side) is the total number of registered voters in the county.

- The "**third**" column is the number of voters who participated in the 2014 primary. *Even though this was the deciding election, fewer than one in seven registered voters bothered to show up.*

- The "**second**" column is the number of votes needed to *win a majority in the controlling party* – in this case, the Republicans.

- There are 166 precincts in Clermont County. One person per precinct can serve on a little known entity called **party central committee.** Central committee members are responsible for deciding which candidates receive endorsements from the party.

- In Clermont, 60% of the central committee – the 100 in the "**first**" column – is the number of central committee votes a candidate needs to receive an endorsement. **This vote is the lynchpin for how the establishment rigs the entire elective process.**

Party endorsements are determined *months before the primary election.* To facilitate this, the local central committee holds an endorsement meeting. *99% of the voting public is unaware that this meeting takes place and the press rarely takes any interest in it.*

Insider candidates, by contrast, are well aware of this meeting and often spend months lobbying the central committee members prior to it to win support.

When the local central committee votes to endorse a candidate, the candidate's name will be included on the **party slate card** or **voter guide.** This guide is distributed to voters before the primary election.

People rely heavily on the party voter guide to help them decide which candidates they will vote for in the primary.

This is even truer during high-profile primaries such as presidential years. Voters come to the polls thinking about the "shiny object" race and <u>not</u> the lower level races. Few people can name the candidates for state rep, state senator, county clerk, commissioners, auditor, local judges, etc. As such, the candidates the party endorses for these offices - and includes on the voter guide - sail through to victory. *Candidates on the party voter guide have a 90%+ chance of winning the primary.*

Central committees (also called "caucuses" in some states) **are the real party establishment.** Insiders and people "in the know" dominate these committees. Often they are elected officials, relatives of elected officials, employees of elected officials, government employees, government contractors, celebrity "stargazers," political "wannabes," and others with substantial conflicts of interest.

Crony and corrupt central committees tend to endorse crony and corrupt candidates for office. These candidates, once elected, vote to enact and uphold crony and corrupt policy. "Garbage in, garbage out."

When the general election comes, the people show up to vote for the party they "lean toward." They have little or no idea how the candidates were really selected and end up rubber-stamping the choices the crony insiders give to them.

Due to the built in one-sidedness of most districts: *he who controls the primary, controls the general.* While no one is looking - and many aren't even bothering to show up - the insiders stack the deck. When the general election finally comes, the establishment candidates win in a manufactured landslide and claim a "mandate" from the people for more of the same.

In steps, here is how the establishment "rigs" elections:

1. Political districts are drawn to strongly favor one of the two major parties in the general election.
2. Crony and corrupt central committees endorse crony and corrupt candidates months *before* the primary.
3. The endorsed candidates' names appear on the party voter guide.
4. The people rely heavily on the party voter guide to decide for whom they will vote.

5. The endorsed candidates win the primary.
6. Due to the lopsided nature of most districts, the primary winners go on to easily win in the general.

As a result of these steps, the cry, "Remember in November!" becomes a siren song for establishment control. *The general election is rendered essentially meaningless because the real choice is made long before the general election ever takes place.*

And, as revealed in the Clermont County graph, 100 local insiders working in almost complete anonymity are able to determine the outcome of the election for 132,966 unsuspecting voters.

(Insert audible gasp here...)

While the details vary by county, with proper focus and engagement, the citizens have the opportunity to change the status quo. They can take back the process of determining whom their candidates, and ultimately, their representatives will be.

The key to doing so is this:

The citizens must take back control of local central committees from the crony and corrupt party establishment.

The central committee system itself is not as much broken as it is neglected. It was designed to be representative and reach all the way down to the neighborhood precinct level.

However, it is only capable of functioning properly if the citizens actively participate in it.

The people must choose central committee representatives who will select and endorse candidates willing to stand for liberty rather than for crony and corrupt establishment interests.

Throw the bums out

The solution to what ails our country is simple. We need to "throw the bums out." *The first to go must be the conflict-of-interest driven individuals inside the local parties.* Only in this way can we truly take back the power of deciding who our representatives will be and, subsequently, determine the direction of our country.

The citizens will never have their voices heard by continuing to "Remember in November" and electing the crony candidates served up to them by the establishment. Instead, the citizens must take the process back at the root - *at the central committee level -* and reclaim the responsibility for choosing their own candidates from the very first steps.

No longer a mystery

The people's lack of awareness of the influence of central committee is a boon to the establishment and helps it maintain its grip on power. Many politicians realize they owe their positions to the establishment and not the people. This greatly diminishes their incentive to listen to or act on behalf of constituents. Hence, the cronies, the corrupt, and the special interests win, and the voice of the people is silenced.

The establishment has done well to keep central committee and its powerful impact out of the limelight, but no more.

A few quick facts:

- In Ohio, there are 9,160 precincts. In general, one person per precinct can serve on his or her county party central committee.

- Central committee positions are determined in the primary election. It usually takes no more than five valid signatures to put your name on the ballot and run.

- Incredibly, and in spite of the enormous influence of central committee, *in roughly one-third of Ohio's precincts, no candidate even files to run for the position.*

- The overwhelming majority of the central committee candidates who are elected run unopposed.

Even where there are vacant central committee seats, the establishment gains the upper hand. This is because vacancies are often filled by "appointment" to other conflict-of-interest driven cronies. Such individuals can be relied on to cast endorsement votes in support of establishment candidates in the future.

No one to blame but ourselves

The door is wide open for the people to take the parties back and regain control of determining who their representatives in government will be.

- Ohio has a population of approximately 11,500,000 people. It would take fewer than 4,000 regular citizens to engage in the central committee process to reclaim a major party from the establishment in our state.

- Nationwide, there are roughly 300,000 precincts. This means 150,001 people engaging in central committees (or in caucuses) could take back a major party from the establishment on a national level.

If the citizens fail to claim these seats, especially since so many are open or uncontested, they have no one to blame but themselves.

You might wonder, if all this is true, why haven't you heard this story before? Why isn't it being shouted from the rooftops? Where is the media? Where are the political pundits and the radio talk show hosts? Why aren't the major donors and the national liberty organizations getting involved?

I wondered the same thing myself when I first heard the story of central committee. I have no rational explanation for the silence of such voices on this topic. Most of those who could easily help drive this message forward and begin substantially moving the needle on reform remain disengaged.

We cannot wait for such people to finally get on board. No one is coming to our rescue. It is up to us. It has always been up to us.

The people need to break free from their old habits about what they believe to be politically impactful. It is time to stop begging and complaining. It is time to stop being reactive and become proactive. *It is time for the citizens to take responsibility for selecting who their candidates for public office will be.*

Restoring the voice of the people

Engaging in the central committee process to effect change is not a wishful or untried theory. Continuing with the example of Clermont County outlined earlier, the citizens in Clermont began working toward winning seats on their local central committee in 2010. By 2014, they achieved a majority in their local party and were able to replace the existing establishment leadership.

Since getting involved, the citizens in Clermont have successfully elected over 150 new liberty-minded people to local office. This includes races for central committee, school boards, township trustee, county level offices, members of the judiciary, and even a new representative to Congress.

Citizens everywhere can similarly assert their voices to hold government accountable and steer our nation on a more productive course. The key is to take back the political parties on a local level and reclaim the candidate selection process from the crony and corrupt establishment.

Part 2: How to Run for Central Committee

Ohio's central committee elections are held during the primary. Elected members of central committee,

- Choose the party leadership
- Approve the party platform
- Approve the party bylaws
- Recommend members to serve on their county board of elections
- Recommend appointments to the judiciary
- Select candidates for endorsement
- Recommend appointments to elected positions vacated before the end of their terms
- Give the party a voice to speak on important policy issues
- Act to provide accolades or censure for elected officials when warranted

A central committee term in Ohio ranges from two to four years. In most cases, being a member of central committee requires a time commitment of less than an hour or two per month.

To run for central committee, generally, a candidate must file with his or her county board of elections three months before the primary. Some counties may require that a candidate collect qualifying petition signatures to run. Usually, no more than five valid signatures are needed.

The first step in running for central committee is to call your local Board of Elections (BOE). Contact your county BOE and ask:

1) **When will the next round of party central committee elections occur in your county?**

2) **What are the requirements to put your name on the ballot and run for your party's central committee?**

Many people worry that political operatives inside the BOE will make it difficult for them to run or try to withhold necessary information. Please put aside this concern. The BOE is there to help candidates file to run. They have a legal obligation to provide you with complete and up-to-date information.

It may be possible to download candidate petition forms online from the Ohio Secretary of State's website. *Be careful! Some forms use legal size paper and are printed front and back. If you print your own form, it should mirror the same formatting as the forms provided by the BOE.*

Filing your candidate petition

Here are a few tips for filing your petition to run. As always, when in doubt, ask your local BOE. It is their job to help you.

- Depending on the county you live in, you may need to collect up to five valid signatures from qualified individuals within your precinct in order to have your name appear on the ballot.
- A candidate cannot sign his or her own petition to count as one of the five signatures needed.
- Some counties do not require you to collect petition signatures. Instead, you may be asked to file an attestation form declaring your intention to run for central committee.
- Before collecting any petition signatures, clearly and completely fill out the TOP of the candidate petition form.
- Once the top of the form is completed, signed, and dated, petition signatures must be collected in correct "date order."
- No signature can appear with a date that is, before the date on the top section of the petition form or out of chronological order with other signatures on the petition signature section.
- A circulator (i.e. the person collecting signatures - most likely you) cannot sign the back of the form with a date that precedes the date on the candidacy section (the

top), or any of the individual petition signatures (the middle).

- If you need five valid signatures, collect more than five. This protects you in case some of the signatures you do collect are determined not qualified by the BOE. But, collect no more than a total of 15 signatures.
- Where possible, collect signatures from people you know to be members of your own party. Independents (NP or NO PARTY registered voters) may be permitted to sign a candidate's petition, but double check with your local BOE.
- The BOE will be able to provide you with your precinct's "walking list" which denotes registered voters in your precinct by street and party designation.
- It is OK to cross out (i.e. run a line through) a signature if someone makes an error such as accidentally writing in the wrong date while they are signing. Have them try again and include the correct information.
- People should sign your petition in the same manner that their signatures appear on BOE records.
- At the bottom of the petition, add up and state the total number of signatures that you intend to submit. For example, if ten people attempted to sign, but you crossed out three due to errors, you would be submitting a total of seven signatures.
- Once you have added up and entered the total number of signatures, complete, sign, and date the bottom of

your form, and return it to the BOE.

Some people worry if they file their petition too early, the party may find someone to run against them. Set aside this concern. Getting your petition completed correctly and assuring your name appears on the ballot is the most important issue. By turning in your petitions a week or two before the deadline, it gives you an opportunity to deal with any errors that may occur with your petition.

As far as the establishment running someone against you; have no fear. There are far more regular citizens than establishment cronies. We probably outnumber them 100 to one. It is very difficult for the establishment to find a puppet in every precinct. The important point is to come at them in mass. Through overwhelming numbers, the people can win a majority on central committee with relative ease.

Write-in candidates

It may be possible to file as a write-in candidate after the initial filing deadline. Write-ins must still file a form at the BOE, if they wish to run. In general, the most effective way to run as a write-in is if no one else bothered to file in your precinct. The BOE will be able to tell you in the days after the initial filing deadline whether anyone filed. The BOE will also have the form you need to complete and be able to tell you the date it needs to be returned (very soon after the initial filing deadline).

If you file as a write-in, be sure to go to the polls and vote for yourself on primary election day. Encourage friends living in your precinct to do so as well. Make sure you write your name on the ballot the same way you filed it on the write-in candidate form at the BOE.

Write-ins are a last resort. It is much easier to win your race if your name appears on the ballot - especially if there is no one else running.

Running to win

Central committee races are the tiniest elections you can imagine. Often only 50 or 60 votes are cast. Once the filing deadline is passed and you are officially on the ballot, you should begin campaigning for your election.

Contact the BOE and find out if you have an opponent. If you are lucky enough to have no opponent, congratulations! Be sure to show up on election day and vote for yourself.

If you do have an opponent, here are some tips to help you win your race:

- Acquire a "walking list" of your precinct from the local BOE. Registered voters will be listed by party (i.e. Republican, Democrat, Libertarian, Green, etc.) and as NP or NO PARTY.

- The walking list is usually arranged alphabetically by street. Look for the households with people who are designated as members of your party.
- Those who share your party designation are the people you want to contact. The fact that they have a party affiliation listed on the walking list indicates a track record of showing up to vote in the primary, which is key.
- Prepare a simple 1 - 2 page letter about why you are running and mail or personally deliver the letter to the households in your precinct (more on this later).
- Include helpful information in your letter about the election, such as: the last day people can register to vote and how they can request and mail in an absentee ballot. Provide online addresses for obtaining absentee ballot request and voter registration forms. List the date of the election along with the address of your precinct's polling location.
- Include the local BOE's phone number, web address, and hours of operation in your letter in case your voters have questions about voting. Your local BOE has all of the timely and accurate information you will need.
- **Do NOT put your letter directly into people's mailboxes**. Think of the mailbox as being charged with 10,000 volts. You may **NOT** put your letter or information directly in a person's mailbox. You may **NOT** hang anything from the mailbox door or flag.

You may **NOT** prop anything between the mailbox's post and the mailbox itself.

- It is OK to rubber band your letter to a mailbox's post (see clear door hanger bags from Uline.com). **But nothing can be placed inside of or touching the physical mailbox itself**. Again, think of it as if it were electric - **NO TOUCHING THE BOX!**

- Many people like to hang their information on their neighbor's doorknobs. This is an excellent technique. Invite others to help you deliver your door-hanger "bags." Sometimes a few teenagers may be willing to help you in exchange for ice cream!

- Be sure to call as many friends living in your precinct as possible and ask them to show up and vote for you. Do this the day of or right before the actual election. Prepare a list of people you can call on election day. "Flushing" out voters in this manner is often the key to winning a close race.

- Plan to stand outside the polls the day of the election to greet voters and pass out cards encouraging people to vote for you. Ask a friend or two to help.

- Be sure to follow the rules about electioneering at the polls. Campaigning inside a polling place or inside the designated boundaries for electioneering is prohibited. Call your local BOE and speak with the polling place election official to be sure you understand and follow the guidelines.

Some people prefer to create a mailing list and contact neighbors about their candidacy through regular mail. Many of your sympathetic voters - i.e. people known to be members of your party - will share the same household. This helps reduce your target list to a more manageable size. Of course, sending regular mail will add some postage expense to your race.

Others prefer going door-to-door and meeting all of their potential voters individually. It is really up to you. I have been elected twice to central committee with staunch opposition both times. I have used a combination of door hangers and personal letters sent through the regular mail. I have never gone door-to-door to get elected. Do what best suits your personal preference.

Reaching out to a handful of friends to help you pass out information can make things a lot easier. Divide up the streets and addresses and have others help you hang your information on doors. By doing so, you will be able to distribute your information very quickly and possibly recruit some devotees to your cause. **Be sure to tell your helpers the rules about never leaving anything in, hanging from, or touching mailboxes!**

Sample letter to your precinct

Essential elements of a good campaign letter are,

- Clearly stating the office you are running for and when the election occurs
- An explanation of *why* you are running
- Defining what central committee is
- Asking people for their vote
- Including your contact information (address, phone, and email)

Here is a sample letter (feel free to use this or modify as you like):

Dear Neighbor,

I am writing you this letter to ask for your vote to be elected as precinct central committee representative to the (your) county, (your) party in the upcoming (election date) primary election.

I am running for this position because I am very concerned about the direction of our country. I believe our nation has accumulated an unacceptable amount of public debt and spends too much on wasteful and ineffective programs. I believe government is growing too rapidly and is making it difficult for our economy to thrive. I believe elected officials should be working to *reduce* the size of government where possible and follow the limited-government guidelines of our Constitution. I believe it is crucial that we elect representatives who will stand on principle, defend the rule of law, protect individual rights, and help restore our country to its core values.

Steering our country on a better course begins with *electing higher quality and more principled representatives to office*. Finding and sending forward such candidates starts at the local party or "county central committee."

As an elected county central committee member it will be my job to help select and support the candidates that run under the name of our party. More than ever, our country needs everyday citizens without conflicts of interest to serve on party central committee. Only in this way can we help improve and uphold our party's integrity.

(A little about you, your work experience, education, values...)

The founders of our country said the people must remain vigilant in order to protect and preserve liberty. Please join me in helping increase the voice of regular citizens inside our party and electing the best possible representatives to office at every level.

If you have questions or would like to contact me, feel free to do so using the information below.

Thank you in advance for your vote on election day!

(Your name, address, phone, and email)

Sample election day handout

As mentioned earlier, many people find it beneficial - and I agree with them - to work outside the polls on election day. Both times I was elected to central committee, I stood outside the polls and handed out postcards with my information asking people to vote for me.

Here is a sample of an election day postcard handout:

(Election date), Elect
Your Name
to (your) Party Central Committee

Most Americans agree our country is on the wrong track. I am running to serve on (your) Party County Central Committee to put principled candidates on future ballots and help correct our nation's course.

I believe in fiscal responsibility, Constitutionally limited government, and free markets. I believe our party should work to elect candidates who believe this too.

**Please vote for me in the primary xx/xx/xxxx
and encourage others to do the same!**

Other helpful tools for running

Here are a few more resources to help you run your central committee race. None of these are required. Use what you like, and leave the rest.

- Set up a free candidate website at: wordpress.com
- Start a free Facebook Page at: facebook.com/pages
- Build a professional email list to stay in touch with voters in your precinct - free for the first 2,000 subscribers at: mailchimp.com
- Start a campaign email address at: gmail.com
- Visit ohioprecinctproject.com/resources for more precinct tools

What if your next central committee election is years away?

After contacting your local BOE, you may discover that the next central committee election in your precinct is several years away. Do not be discouraged by this. Begin working in and developing your precinct *before* the next central committee election.

Here are a few things you can do if your next central committee election is years away.

- Deliver a personal letter to voters in your precinct providing valuable information about "how to participate" before every election. Contact your local BOE to acquire all the accurate and relevant information you will need.
- Inform voters about when early voting begins. Tell them when and how they can request and submit an absentee ballot.
- Ask your local BOE about acquiring voter registration and absentee voter request forms to distribute along with your letter. *Over time this can greatly improve new voter registration and overall voter participation in your precinct!*
- Provide voters with the address of your precinct's polling location and indicate the hours it will be open on election day.

- Inform voters how they can contact the local BOE with questions about voting. Include the BOE's web address, phone number, and hours of operation.
- Put up yard signs at key neighborhood intersections on election day that say, "Vote Today!" to remind people to participate.
- Whenever possible, attend the local meetings of your county central committee as a guest.

Such activity is well worth the effort. It advances the overall cause and makes winning your future election a whole lot easier. By the time the next central committee election occurs in your area, voters in your precinct will know you to be a trustworthy and valuable resource.

Part 3: Winning your Township or County

Central committee politics is a "winner take all" contest. Getting control of the chairmanship or "the gavel" is the key. Whoever controls the gavel gets to make most of the decisions and represents the voice of the majority on central committee in your area. Sometimes achieving this goal may take a few election cycles.

When the citizens in my county got started with central committee engagement, in 2010, we took it one step at a time. For my part in the effort, I began by focusing on winning the local township in which I live. At the time there were 42 precincts in the township and roughly 29 of them were "open" (i.e. no candidate filed to run). We recruited 26 regular-citizen candidates, with many of them running in the open precincts. When the election was over, we won 23 seats. This was far more than the establishment had on their side, only around thirteen.

After the election, we held a "reorganization meeting" as required by the county party bylaws. At the meeting, we elected new township leadership (i.e. chairman, vice-chairman, treasurer, and secretary). In less than an hour, we swept away the old guard and put the citizens in control.

Winning in your local area

Here are a few tips for winning your township or county:

- Check with your local BOE (or visit their website) and research how many precincts there are in your area.
- Determine the number of seats required to win a majority. Add a few extra to the number, just to be safe. For example, if there are 50 seats total and 26 are needed for a majority, try to win 30 or 35.
- Ask the BOE how many precincts had NO candidate file to run for your party's central committee in the last election. These seats are ripe for the taking. This is where the people outnumbering the cronies comes into direct play. The establishment has a very hard time finding a person willing to serve as their minion in every precinct.
- Look back a few election cycles and break down your area's precincts into three categories: **open** (no one filed to run), **uncontested** (only one candidate filed to run), and **contested** (one or more candidates filed to run in the same precinct).

Recruiting candidates

As noted earlier, the easiest seats to win are the open seats. Obtain a copy of the walking list for each open precinct you have identified.

- Get together with friends, local community group members, church members, liberty-group members, etc. and search for people living in target precincts you can invite to run.
- If you exhaust all your outlets to recruit candidates, you can try sending postcards to people in the precincts you are targeting. Ask people to come to an informational meeting about running for this important position.
- If none of the above works, take a friend and a walking list, and go door-to-door recruiting candidates.

All of the above techniques have been used successfully at one time or another. The first time we engaged in our county, out of 200 precincts, we won about 50 races. The second time we engaged, the number of precincts had been reduced during apportionment to 166. This time we found 119 people to run out of the 166 seats and won 100 of these races. As a result, the citizens took majority control of the local party and installed new leadership.

Remember, the citizens greatly outnumber the establishment. It is very difficult for the insiders to find a crony willing to sell out his or her country for self-interest in every precinct. But, it is very easy to find a liberty-loving citizen. Going toe-to-toe, we win. The challenge is to teach the relatively unknown concept of central committee to enough people and encourage them to step up and serve.

The good news is, when people hear the whole story, most are eager to get involved.

At home and local meetings

When you identify individuals who are willing to learn more about running, it is very helpful to set up group meetings in homes or at local venues to discuss the overall effort. This is a good place for people to ask questions and work together on strategies to recruit other candidates and build even more momentum. It is very rare, after such meetings, for people to decide not to get involved.

A good technique to use at a group meeting is to pass out printed copies of target precinct walking lists and ask, "Does anyone know a person living in these areas?" Highlight the names of prospects and make a plan to call them. One local organizer in my county held a phoning party on his back porch. Volunteers brought their cell phones, had some wine and cheese, and dialed away. This proved very effective. Using such creative and fun techniques, you should able to assemble a sufficient list of people to run.

Don't go it alone

Work together with others in your county to understand what is required to run, how to complete and file petitions, and run a campaign. Many times people with uncontested races will be able to lend a hand to those who have challengers. Many hands make the work light!

When I first engaged in my township, we all used the same template for postcards and handouts. We also helped each other assemble our target voter lists. A collaborative effort prevents anyone from having to reinvent the wheel and promotes greater opportunity for success.

Part 4: After the Election

Once your election is over, there are two possible outcomes,

1) Some people win their elections, but not enough to establish a majority
2) Enough people win their elections to establish a majority

If you do not win a majority, you may still be able to change the party leadership. This requires building a coalition with current party members. There are always a few legitimate non-cronies currently serving inside most local parties. Connecting with these people can be very helpful. Other groups have found success by sending a letter to the elected members of their central committee that includes a mission statement and an invitation to work together.

Mention in your letter to the elected central committee members that the coalition you and others are building intends to:

- Stand on principle and not cronyism or "stargazing" (i.e. fascination with access to 'celebrity' politicians).
- Meet regularly and take vetting, selecting, and endorsing candidates seriously.
- Vote to endorse and support candidates in the primary because, if you don't, someone else will. **Neutrality on**

endorsements is NOT a nod to fair play. It is a gift to outside special interests, candidates with high name recognition, candidates with money, and "out-of-towners" who want to control the outcome of elections in your area.

- Rewrite the party by-laws, if necessary, to re-empower the elected precinct representatives. This includes eliminating voting rights for phony "at large" or "lifetime" committee members, and the removal of any provisions to include "automatic" voting rights for incumbent elected officials. Such crony-supporting schemes dilute and usurp the voice of the legitimately elected precinct representatives.
- Adopt a party platform if one has not been adopted in the past.
- Vote to speak directly on important issues. For example, issuing formal resolution statements to reject policies like Common Core and Obamacare expansion.
- Vote to publicly censure elected officials who usurp the core principles of the party through their actions.
- Vote to publicly commend elected officials for standing strong on principle and acting in accordance with the party platform.

The reorganization meeting

By law, county parties must hold reorganization meetings to elect new party leadership shortly after the election results of the primary are certified. *It is very important that you meet with other newly elected central committee members **before** the reorganization meeting to discuss your game plan.*

If you think you have the number of votes required to choose new party leadership, you should decide who those leaders are going to be **in advance of the reorganization meeting.**

Central committee meetings in Ohio are generally administered using Roberts Rules of Order. It is very important to study and understand these rules *before* attending the reorganization meeting. There are many resources available to help you learn the rules including books from Amazon and YouTube videos you can watch. It is crucial that you understand how to work within Robert's Rules of Order to protect your new coalition from being railroaded by procedure.

Coordinate who will "nominate" the individuals you want to elect for the various positions and decide who will "second" the nomination. Practice calling "point of order" to slow the process down, if needed. Practice motions to "call for a vote." Knowing who your leadership candidates are and how you will manage the procedural elements *before* the reorganization meeting takes place is absolutely essential.

When the reorganization meeting occurs, it will be opened and initially run by the incumbent chairperson or his or her surrogate.

A few tips about the reorganization meeting,

- Do not allow any significant decisions to be made by "voice vote." This prevents the chairperson from subjectively saying, "the ayes have it" on an important vote.
- Insist on confidential paper ballots and have several people oversee the counting of the ballots.
- Be careful of calls to vote for a "slate" of new leadership. Instead, vote for each leadership position individually. Doing so helps keep the process controlled, even-paced, and deliberate.

As much as possible, be sure only elected central committee members are those deciding the reorganization votes. In one instance, non-central committee members were permitted to attend the local reorganization meeting. When the former chairperson called for a voice vote for a "slate" of leadership candidates, the general crowd erupted in "ayes." The chairperson then gave leadership control back to the incumbents. Don't let this happen to you. This is combat, albeit, procedural combat. Be prepared to fight and win.

Lastly, it may be a good idea to bring a video camera (cell

40

phone cameras will do) to the reorganization meeting to record any attempted shenanigans that may take place. It makes for some great reality TV and training film for later. As my friend and central committee mentor Rick Herron likes to point out, "You can't pay for entertainment like this. They ought to charge admission!"

Recruit a parliamentarian

One great way to ensure meetings run smoothly is to enlist the services of a "parliamentarian." A parliamentarian is a person who clearly understands Robert's rules and whose specific job is to see that the rules are adhered to. This person can prevent bullies or outspoken individuals from taking advantage of others who are unfamiliar with the procedures. Ideally, the parliamentarian should also be knowledgeable of the party bylaws and state regulations applying to party central committees.

Part 5: State Central Committee

State central committees select and endorse statewide candidates for office such as: Governor, Auditor, Treasurer, Secretary of State, Attorney General, State School Boards, and State Supreme Court. They are also responsible for sending two representatives to serve on the national party committees (i.e. RNC for Republicans, DNC for Democrats).

One of the most important aspects of taking back county central committees is the power they have to endorse principled representatives to serve on state central committee.

There are 33 state senate districts in Ohio. Each district elects two representatives, one male and one female, to their respective state party central committee for a total of 66 seats. The elections are run in the primary and occur every two years. So, for the citizens to win a majority on a state party central committee, it takes winning 34 seats. This is a very easy race to enter. There is no filing fee and it has many similar characteristics to running a race for county central committee. Contact your local BOE to learn more about the requirements to run for your party's state central committee.

The establishment controls state central committee with money. In the past, they have spent hundreds of thousands of dollars to mail postcards in support of their chosen state central committee candidates. I have even seen unsuspecting voters carrying these postcards into the polls on election day. Do not be deterred by this! *Every state senate district in Ohio should have at least two regular citizen challengers to step up and run.*

In fact, given the ease of entry to these races, *there is no excuse for not finding two good people per party willing to at least give this a try in each of the 33 senate districts.* Work together to assist the candidates you support for state central committee. Everyone with an individual central committee race should simultaneously be helping the state central committee candidates win their elections.

Defeating the establishment mailers

Defeating the establishment and their mailings is simple. By taking back the county parties, it creates the necessary infrastructure to endorse and advance liberty-minded state central committee candidates in the future. A healthy county party working to support its endorsed candidates is far more powerful than crony-created postcards mailed from miles away.

Another way to help win is through new media. It is easier than ever to spread the word online about liberty candidates. *It is the duty of everyone to help identify the liberty representatives and to spread the word about them to others via blogs, email, and social media.* Dictators with tanks and fighter jets have been taken down using online outreach. Surely we can use the same tools to defeat a bunch of self-interested political toadies.

Conclusion

If you look at it objectively, it should be no surprise to anyone
that the political parties have come to be controlled by insiders
who benefit from bigger and bigger government. This is an
unintended consequence that has occurred over time. It isn't
some vast conspiracy. It just happened. There is no point in
getting angry about it or staging massive protests to overhaul
and remake the system. The sooner we see this situation for
what it really is, the better equipped we will be to take
constructive action to address the problem.

*The cronies gravitated to the one place where they could exert the most
influence to serve their personal interests; the central committees of the
political parties.*

In hindsight, for them, this was tactically brilliant.

1. The cronies, with direct incentive for personal gain,
   showed up to take control of the parties.
2. The people, busy living their lives or focused on other
   more conventional but politically ineffective outlets,
   easily gave up this control.
3. Corrupt, crony party members support and advance
   corrupt, crony candidates.
4. Corrupt, crony candidates, once elected, implement
   and uphold corrupt, crony policies.

5. The people, harmed by these policies, seek to exercise their Constitutional right to "throw the bums out" on election day.

6. Unwittingly, the representatives the voters elect are either the same or a different set of cronies drawn from one or the other party's crony basket.

7. The change people hope to see does not materialize. In fact, many times, quite the opposite happens. (i.e. Ohio Republicans with 100% control of state government have increased state spending nearly 40% since 2011, opposed passing a right to work law, voluntarily expanded Obamacare, and are fully implementing Common Core in our state).

8. The people lose faith in the process. They quit their party and go "independent." They fail to show up at primary election time. They say the system is broken and give up.

9. *As more and more well-meaning people head for the exits, the cronies consolidate an even greater amount of power and the cycle continues.*

10. Lather, rinse, repeat.

The good news, however, is that the door is wide open for the citizens to take the parties back and break this cycle. By endorsing and electing principled candidates who will implement responsible, freedom-friendly policy, the system can be peacefully repaired and its integrity restored.

When I consider the fact that nearly a third of Ohio's central committee positions go unfilled and most run unopposed, rather than despair over the lack of participation by the people, I see an enormous opportunity for a positive change in the status quo.

Focus on one thing

Where do we go from here? No discipline exists in a vacuum. *We need to stop spending time on things that make no difference and start spending time on things that do.*

A few places to start,

- Turn off cable TV news
- Turn off talk radio
- Cancel your subscription to the newspaper
- Uninstall your Drudge app
- Stop paying attention to tabloid political news
- Stop attending rallies
- Stop writing letters to the editor
- Stop begging someone else's crony representative to do the right thing

Use all the time you save to focus on taking back both your neighborhood precinct and your county central committee.

Later, if you want to go back and do some of the old political stuff you used to do, go ahead.

But not before!

The power of central committee engagement is real and is unmatched in its impact. It is the key to reestablishing the voice of the people in the political process and restoring our political system to health.

There is no better place to begin such an important effort to correct our nation's course than right here in America's most important swing state.

So, stop by your local BOE today to pick up your candidate petition and start spreading the word to others.

In Liberty,

Ted Stevenot

Glossary of Central Committee Related Terms

Appointment - This is when the current central committee fills an "open seat." This can occur because no one bothered to file to run for the seat or due to a resignation. Depending on the county bylaws, a party chairman may directly determine an appointment or the decision may be made by a vote of the county central committee members. Appointments by the establishment open the door for the deck to be stacked in favor of the cronies. This can have a huge impact in determining the outcome of future endorsement votes. Some county parties give preference when deciding appointments to individuals who physically reside in an open precinct, while others may not.

BOE or Board of Elections - This is the government agency in every county responsible for administering local elections. Ohio has 88 counties and therefore 88 BOEs. The individuals serving on these county boards are not adversaries, but are there to help. In very rare instances, any problem you may encounter with your local BOE can generally be resolved with the help of the Secretary of State's office in Columbus.

Candidate Attestation - In the context of central committee, this is a form filed on or before the candidate filing deadline that attests an individual's desire to appear on the ballot and run for a particular party's central committee. These forms play a role when there is no requirement to obtain candidate petition signatures. This process varies by county. To find out the requirements in your area, check with your local BOE.

Candidate Petition Forms - These are the official forms used to declare candidacy for central committee. Depending on your county, qualifying petition signatures may or may not be required. The appropriate candidate form must be completed correctly and returned to the BOE on or before the filing deadline. Check with your local BOE to determine the exact requirements and which form must be used in your area.

Censure - This is a powerful tool that can be used by state and county central committees to reprimand a party candidate or elected official for violating the party's principles. Usually drafted and voted on by the committee members, censures may be posted online or issued via press release to the media.

Central Committee - This is the true party establishment. Parties are no more than the people who serve inside them. *"People are policy. If you want to change the policy, you have to change the people in charge."* The power of central committees to endorse candidates is monumental and it is the key to electing liberty-minded candidates to office. Serving on central committee does not require a large time commitment, but makes a dramatic difference in restoring the health of our political system.

Circulator - This is a person who collects and submits candidate petition signatures. A circulator swears that he or she has personally witnessed the petition signatures and attests to the total number of signatures being submitted.

Closed Meeting - Under certain circumstances, central committee meetings may be closed to the public. Other meetings may be open to the public as required by law.

Contested Seat - This is when two or more people run for the same central committee seat. Most central committee seats run either uncontested or no candidate bothers to file.

County Board of Elections - See BOE.

County Central Committee - Party central committees are established at the county level. Below the county level there may be township committees, wards, or other municipal delineations. However, all of these subgroups are members of the county central committee. County committees typically select and endorse candidates for races encompassed by their geographical area.

Electioneering - This refers to candidate or issue campaign activity occurring outside of a voter polling location on election day. Election officials typically measure and designate an official physical distance from the polling location in which electioneering may legally occur. Electioneering is prohibited inside a polling location and within the designated boundaries. Check with your local BOE to determine the exact rules in your area.

Endorsement - This is the prize a candidate wins if he or she receives enough votes at the central committee endorsement meeting. In most instances, it means the candidate's name will appear on the party "slate card" or "voter guide" that is distributed before the election. People rely heavily on the party slate card to help them decide for whom they will vote. Every county should take responsibility for endorsing candidates and defending their local slate card. If you don't pick your candidates, it opens the door for someone else to choose your candidates for you. When this happens, the representative voice of the local voters goes unheard.

Endorsement Meeting - This is the meeting in which qualifying members of the local central committee vote to determine candidate endorsements. It is important that only elected and legitimately appointed members of the central committee decide these votes. These individuals are intended to represent the voice of voters in each precinct. Bogus schemes to empower "lifetime" executive committees, automatically include incumbent elected officials, or other non-precinct level representatives in endorsement votes generally serves to empower the establishment and usurp the will of the people.

Executive Committee - These are the individuals chosen by the members of the central committee to lead the local party. It is very important that the true representatives of the voters determine who these party leaders will be.

General Election - This is the November election. In districts drawn to be controlled by one or the other major party (i.e. gerrymandered), the controlling party's candidates will be "safe" victories on general election day. *In such areas, the primary election may provide the only realistic opportunity to make a change in representation.* Victory in the primary is strongly influenced by the local party slate card or voter guide. Whether or not a candidate's name appears on the primary election voter guide is generally determined by an endorsement vote of the local central committee. This process may vary somewhat by county.

Gerrymandering - This refers to the drawing of political district lines to favor one or the other major political party. The term is a combination of a last name "Gerry" and the word "salamander." Elbridge Gerry (1744 - 1814) was a signer of the Declaration of Independence and the Articles of Confederation. As governor of Massachusetts, Gerry signed a bill into law apportioning certain state political districts in favor of his own party. One of the districts was said to resemble a salamander. Hence the term "gerrymander" was born.

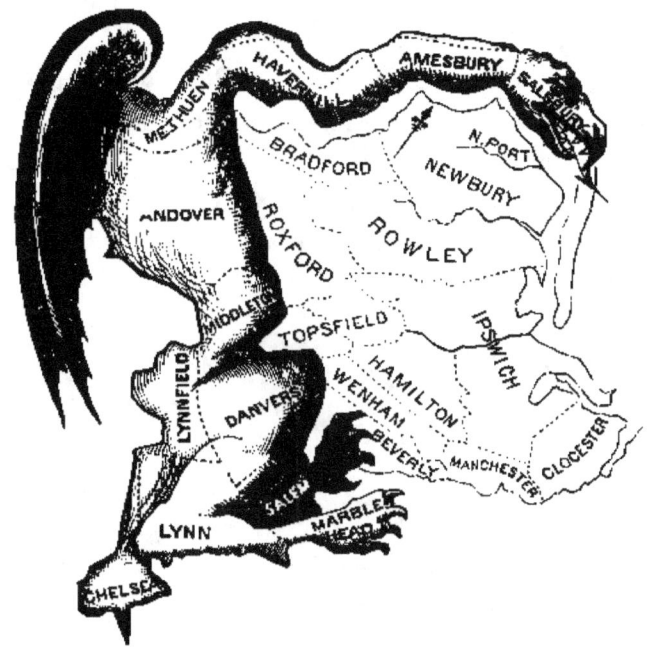

"*Printed in March 1812, this political cartoon was drawn in reaction to the newly drawn state senate election district of South Essex created by the Massachusetts legislature to favor the Democratic-Republican Party candidates of Governor Elbridge Gerry over the Federalists.*"

Source: https://en.wikipedia.org/wiki/Gerrymandering

National Committee - This refers to the national committee of a political party. Many are familiar with the terms "Democratic

National Committee" and "Republican National Committee" or "DNC" and "RNC." Few are aware that such committees may take shape and form all the way down to the neighborhood precinct level. The details differ by state, but each state party is responsible for sending delegates to their respective national committees. These national committees determine party leadership, party platforms, and the rules for choosing candidates in important races such as President of the United States.

Open Meeting - This is a meeting of the central committee that is open to the public. Central committee meetings, such as those to determine the temporary replacement of certain partisan elected officials due to resignation or death, may be mandated to be open to the public and the press. Other meetings may be closed to the public at the discretion of the local committee or committee chairperson.

Open Precinct - This is a neighborhood precinct in which no candidate filed to run for central committee. Roughly one-third of the central committee seats in Ohio are open because no one bothers to file. After the primary election and the reorganization meeting have occurred, open seats are often filled by appointment. Open precincts are very advantageous to the establishment as the positions can be filled with "insiders" such as government employees, government contractors, family members of elected officials, and others with similar conflicts of interest. Such individuals can generally be counted on to support establishment candidates during endorsement votes.

Parliamentarian - This is a person who acts as a third party voice in meetings to help ensure that procedures are followed correctly. A parliamentarian should be impartial. His or her only purpose is to see that the rules are properly adhered to. This person should be well versed in Robert's Rules of Order, the party bylaws, and any applicable state laws that relate to the activities of central committee.

Partisan Race - This is an election in which party designations appear alongside the names of candidates. In the general election, judicial candidates are not designated by party affiliation. Issuing and distributing a party slate card serves as a critical guide for voters in such races.

Party Bylaws - These are the rules for the operation of each individual party entity. The duly elected and appointed members of each central committee should determine the bylaws. County parties in Ohio often establish their own unique sets of local bylaws. The same goes for state central committees on a national level. It is the responsibility of the people to gain control of the process of determining party bylaws to ensure that their voices will be heard in the candidate selection and endorsement process. Gaining such control requires winning at least a majority of the elected central committee seats.

Party Chairperson - This individual should be chosen by the duly elected members of the central committee. He or she wields the gavel. This person generally serves as the spokesperson on behalf of the local party. The party chairperson may also decide who leads various party subcommittees.

Party Platform - This is a statement of the principles and beliefs for which the party stands. A party platform, similar to a corporate mission statement, is critical to maintaining the integrity of the party. Adherence to a well-founded party platform assures that party members and party elected officials will be guided by a set of principles rather than by individual personalities.

Party Secretary - This person keeps the minutes of meetings and maintains an up-to-date roster of appointed and elected central committee members. He or she is generally responsible for publicizing and informing members about the meeting schedule. This person may also help facilitate communication between candidates seeking endorsement and current central committee members. The party secretary is generally chosen by a vote of the duly elected members of the central committee at the reorganization meeting.

Primary Election - This is the election in which voters "choose" the candidates to represent their party in the general election. The process varies widely by state. In Ohio, fewer than one-in-four registered voters, on average, bothers to participate in the primary election. Due to gerrymandering, the primary may be the only opportunity for voters to make a change in representation in their district. In one-party controlled districts, *"He who controls the primary, controls the general."* This sets up party endorsements and the party slate card as indispensable resources for determining which candidate will ultimately be elected to office.

Reorganization Meeting - This is the meeting that occurs soon after the primary election in which central committee races appeared on the ballot. At the reorganization meeting, newly elected central committee members vote to decide party leadership (i.e. Chairperson, Vice Chairperson, Secretary, Treasurer). This is a "winner take all" contest. It is similar to what happens in legislative bodies like the house and senate. The goal is to "get the gavel" and win the party chairmanship.

Resolution - This is a policy statement made publicly by the members of a central committee. It should be consistent with the principles of the party as detailed in the party platform. Resolution statements are used as a means of protecting the integrity of the party. For example, "Be it resolved the ABC county Republican Party formally rejects the federal intrusion into local education known as Common Core..." Such a statement should go on to define how the principles of the party shape the position being taken on the given topic. Resolution statements assure citizens that the party remains grounded in principles and help guide elected officials in determining which policies they should or should not support.

Robert's Rules of Order - This is a common set of guidelines intended to provide organized structure and facilitate responsible deliberation in group meetings. Robert's Rules are used throughout our political system as well as in many business and civic organizations. It is very important to learn these rules to ensure that your voice will be heard and that meetings proceed in an orderly manner and with civil decorum.

Safe District - This is a political district that has been drawn to favor one or the other major party in the general election. Political lines are generally redrawn every ten years, after the Census, to apportion districts by population. This happens for both state and federal districts. Political parties have been manipulating the mapping of district lines to serve their interests since the early 1800s. Competitive districts can be very costly to the parties and provide unwanted uncertainty in reelecting incumbents. It is unlikely the establishment ever imagined members of their own parties would turn this system against them in the name of reform. Safe districts provide an open opportunity for citizens to throw out crony, establishment candidates and elect principled representatives in their stead.

Secretary of State - This is the top election official in every state. The Secretary of State's office is an excellent resource for information about elections, campaign finance, rules pertaining to voting, historical voter data, candidate filing requirements, and more. The employees of the Secretary of State's office are there to help you. When in doubt, call and ask either your county board of elections (BOE) or the Secretary of State's office for assistance with any questions you may have about running for office or advocating in elections.

Slate Card (or Voter Guide) - This is the list of candidates endorsed by the party that is distributed to voters prior to the election. Voters rely heavily on the party slate card to decide for whom they will vote. Candidates whose names appear on the party slate card during the primary election have an extremely high probability of winning their races.

State Central Committee - This entity functions much like a county party, but on the state level. State central committee seats are determined by state senate district. There are 33 state senate districts in Ohio. One man and one woman from each senate district may serve, thereby, deriving a total of 66 state central committee seats per party. State central committees decide endorsements for state level positions such as Governor, Treasurer, Secretary of State, Attorney General, Auditor, State Supreme Court Justices, and potentially many other races. They are also responsible for determining the state party bylaws and adopting the state party platform. State central committee seats are currently decided every two years during the primary. State central committee members elect the state party chairman and send delegates to the national party committees. *It should be the goal of the regular citizens in both major parties to see that these committees are made up of individuals who represent the will of the people rather than the crony establishment.*

Uncontested Seat - This refers to a central committee seat that is elected without opposition. Most central committee seats are elected on an uncontested basis. This reflects the lack of awareness on the part of the citizens about the existence and influence of central committees. Liberty-minded individuals who care about the direction of the country should be challenging incumbents for these seats. No one "owns" his or her seat on central committee and there is a reason why we have designated terms of service. Healthy competition at the ballot box amplifies the voice of the people and promotes the overall integrity and accountability of the central committee system.

Voter Guide - See Slate Card.

Walking List - This is a list of registered voters, by precinct, that is available from your local BOE. Walking lists are public record and are generally arranged alphabetically by street name. Walking lists are of assistance to candidates and others for determining how voters align by party on a precinct level. They can also be helpful in indicating which individuals historically choose to participate in primary elections.

About the Author:

Ted Stevenot has been involved in Ohio's grassroots liberty movement since 2009. He has served as president of two of the state's largest liberty organizations and is a founding member of the Ohio Precinct Project, an initiative to promote greater citizen involvement in party central committee.

Ted can be reached at:
tedstevenot.com